THE FOLLY
Settle's house of mystery

Peter Brears and Richard Hoyle
with illustrations by Peter Brears

North Craven Building Preservation Trust
2018

Published by North Craven Building Preservation Trust, The Folly, Victoria Street, Settle, North Yorkshire, BD24 9EY. © 2018 North Craven Building Preservation Trust.

Front cover photograph by Antony Sharratt © North Craven Building Preservation Trust; Figure 1 courtesy North Yorkshire Record Office; Figures 3–11, 13 and 23 © Peter Brears; Figure 12 courtesy Catherine Glover, Figure 17, 'The West Front of The Folly' by Richard Carman © Richard Carman, Figure 21 Crown Copyright Historic England Archive, BB71-14549 (EP6423-1050). All other pictures are drawn from the collections of the North Craven Building Preservation Trust.

ISBN 978-0-9504075-2-4

Designed by Carnegie Book Production

Printed by Short Run Press

THE FOLLY: SETTLE'S HOUSE OF MYSTERY

If you walk a few yards out of Settle market place, past the Talbot Inn, then you will catch sight of one of the architectural treasures of the Yorkshire Dales. This is The Folly, a late seventeenth-century townhouse. Today it acts as a museum and heritage centre for Settle and north Craven but for most of its history it has never served the purpose for which it was built, as a prestige residence for a Settle lawyer. It makes a statement not only through its size but the amount of glazing it contains, and the novelty of corner windows. Contemporaries must have been impressed, and so should we.

For long periods the building lacked a use in line with its size and grandeur. It has been tenements, workshops and for a time a farmhouse. Only in the 1970s was it restored to its original purpose as a gentleman's residence, but since then it has been – for short periods – an antiques shop and holiday let. That it has been so many things perhaps explains why so much of the house survives in the form it was built, or had taken by early in the eighteenth century.

Why a house of mystery? We know who the builder was and his occupation. He was *the* Settle solicitor of his age, a man called Richard Preston. There are hints of a troubled life: he died a relatively young man without leaving a will (and so probably unexpectedly). The house was both his home and his office: its site and scale were to flaunt his success. And yet the last years of his life were marked by a degree of professional disgrace and Preston's inventory suggests that at the time of his death the house was only partly furnished. We have a datestone

3

1 A bill from Richard Preston's legal practice, dated 17 September 1689, with his signature. North Yorkshire Record Office, ZXC I/5/5.

over the door but not even this is quite certain. The date has been worn away by the weather. Is it 1675 or 1679? Whichever it is, it poses a problem. How did Preston find the money to build a sizeable house so early in his career? More than this though, is the house we see today the one that Preston built? We have a room-by-room inventory of its contents made after Preston's death in early 1696 but this includes no rooms on the top floor. Does this mean that the house was unfinished at the time of Preston's death and only took its familiar form later? Or is there some other explanation as to why the men who made the inventory never ventured up to the top floor?

So whilst we know a great deal, aspects of the house remain ... mysterious.

Richard Preston appears to have been born in Long Preston in 1643 and first appears as a lawyer in Settle in the early 1670s (**1**).* He was therefore building his house in Settle when he was in his early thirties. It has not been possible to discover when he married, but his wife was called Lettice and his daughters – Margaret, Lettice and Millicent

* Numbers in bold refer to the illustrations.

– were baptised at Giggleswick in 1672, 1674 and 1676 respectively. Preston himself died in January 1696 and was buried at Giggleswick on 2 February 1696. His widow and daughters retained the house until 1703 when Preston's lands were partitioned between his daughters and their husbands.

The house formed part of the share of the vicar of Giggleswick, Richard Ellershaw and his wife Margaret: within a month they had sold it to Margaret Dawson widow and her son, William Dawson gent. It has been suggested that Dawson practised as a lawyer in Settle, but moved to Langcliffe Hall when his grandfather died in 1712. His first wife died in 1708, and Dawson remarried in 1720. He settled The Folly on his son by his second wife and the junior line of the Dawsons retained ownership until Philip Dawson, the last of the name, sold it in 1983. From the moment William Dawson moved to Langcliffe until the mid-1960s the house was never used as a gentleman's residence. We can guess that it was for this reason that it came to be known as The Folly. In addition, stories circulated at a much later date that its builder had beggared himself in building the house, that it was, in effect, a monument to individual folly. This seems not to be true, but it makes a good story.

The reason why no one of status lived in the house after about 1720 is that the house was built for a purpose, and lost that purpose. We might usefully see The Folly as a house over a lawyer's offices. For that reason it has two entrances – a 'public' or professional entrance through a monumental (if not actually gross) doorway which led into an open hall with an ostentatious fireplace, and a much more discreet, private entrance that led into the family's kitchen and service rooms on the ground floor, with a private backstairs to their bedrooms above. There was a connecting door between the two ground floor halves of the house to the right of the fireplace in the hall, itself a discreet piece of work, almost concealed (**13** and **14**). It seems most likely that clients or visitors coming through the main door would come into a large light room in which Preston's clerks worked. Preston himself almost certainly used the south corner room with its expanse of glazing as his private room: it was into this room that clients might be called to discuss their affairs. This mixture of the professional and the domestic explains many of the odd features of the house.

It also explains the site. If The Folly now seems to be tucked away in a back street of Settle (**2**), it needs to be remembered that the road running down the hill from Upper Settle past The Folly's front door was the road from Skipton to Kendal – the king's highway – until the turnpike was made in the 1750s. In the fullness of time this new approach to Settle reorientated the town. It should also be remembered that until gentlemen's houses began to appear in Duke Street in the later eighteenth century, The Folly had a clear aspect towards the west. (It is all part of The Folly's fall that buildings were erected so close to it.) This then was a prestigious site even though it was an awkward one, requiring a house which was all width and height and little depth: but if this was perhaps less than ideal, it allowed for a building with an imposing façade and copious windows.

SETTLE . THE FOLLY.

43787

2 View of the Folly, *c.* 1910.
Note the two figures at the
south end, the man standing
and a woman peering round
the corner of the building.

8

3 Although intending the house to be much taller, at first Richard Preston built only the lower storeys with a temporary roof, keeping in store the corner stones and mullioned windows he had prepared for the upper storeys. The house would then have looked something like this, familiar and yet strange.

Building a house of this impressive scale and appearance was an expensive undertaking, and it seems likely that it was beyond Preston's means. There are aspects of the house that suggest economy. It seems likely that some of the walls of a building already standing on the site were reused at the back. The carved masonry is of highest quality but the masonry of the walls is of unshaped stone. Preston restricted the finest display of huge glass windows, finely-carved masonry and high-quality carpentry to those parts seen by the passing public and visitors; the façade and the interior of the hall, including the lower flight of its grand staircase. Horizontal breaks in the masonry running just above the first-floor string course of the front wall, and also along the back wall, show that initially Preston's house had a simple ridged roof over the first floor. Fine masonry for the window mullions and perhaps the quoins for the corner of the second floor were prepared, but remained unused until the additional storey was added at a later date. For a time, the building looked very different to the one that exists today (**3**).

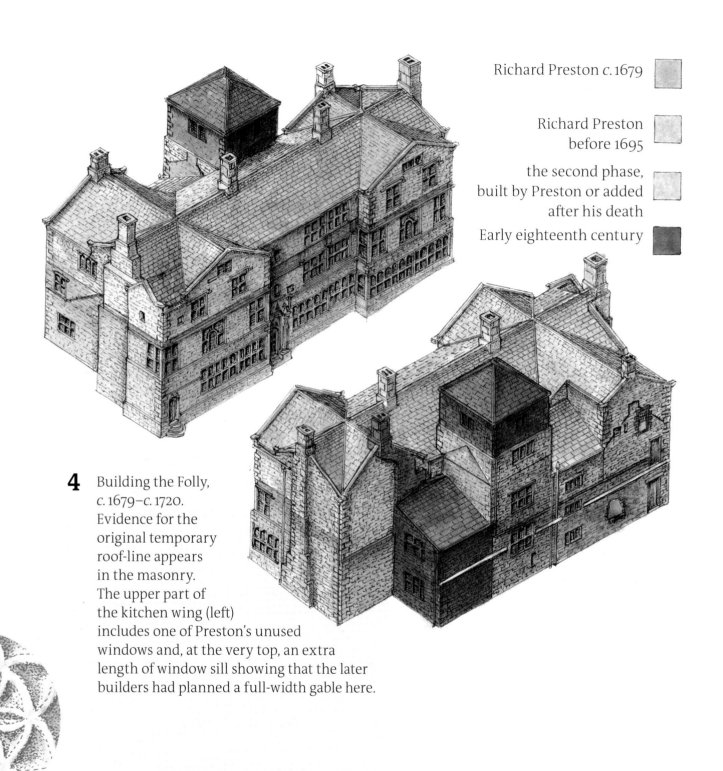

Richard Preston *c.*1679

Richard Preston before 1695

the second phase, built by Preston or added after his death

Early eighteenth century

4 Building the Folly, *c.*1679–*c.*1720. Evidence for the original temporary roof-line appears in the masonry. The upper part of the kitchen wing (left) includes one of Preston's unused windows and, at the very top, an extra length of window sill showing that the later builders had planned a full-width gable here.

The attic storey was built to a lower standard. Its windows were much plainer, the fine mullions retained for its construction being turned back-to-front in the north gable to match cruder ones at this level. The carpentry is similarly crude, and there are no original fireplaces. Take here the two gables at the north and south ends of the building. These are charmingly irregular: the one at the south end (to the right as you look at The Folly) is larger and is over a three light window: it extends to the end wall of the building. The one at the north stops short of the north wall and sits over a two light window, but the fact that a window sill three lights wide remains in situ and the corresponding lintel was broken to fit suggests that the two gables were intended to have the same shape and that the northern one was, for some reason, curtailed. (This can be seen if you look at Figure 2). A taking-in or loading door at the back of the north wing was also provided for raising and lowering goods from the yard below

and this prompts the suggestion that at some time the top floor was used for warehousing or even textile production.

It is also possible that the completion of the building led to more internal remodelling than has been appreciated. In its first form the building may just have had staircases at both ends. The hall may have been built with a high blank wall on its east side. (This is the layout shown in (6)). The staircase may have been inserted at the time the second floor was added, with a staircase tower being built at the back of the building to contain it. At a later date still a small tower or viewing room topped the staircase tower.

So what looks like an idiosyncratic building of a single date turns out to have been built in four stages as shown in (4) with the possibility that the builder's initial concept was never fulfilled in his lifetime. But if he ran out of money, he also had £700 lent out on mortgage at the time he died so he was not poor.

If all of this suggests that Preston died with the house incomplete, then it is a mystery as to when and by whom it was completed. Once the paterfamilias was dead, the income would have ceased to flow and it hardly seems likely that his widow would have had the inclination to extend an already substantial house. It is possible that some additions were made by William Dawson – it has been suggested that the tower above the stairwell at the rear of the house is his work – and it is at least plausible that he purchased a house which was only partly finished and brought it to completion. The truth is that we will probably never know. We can be confident that the house had taken its familiar form by the time Samuel Buck drew Settle from a distance around 1720: The Folly can be seen standing above the town, under Castleberg, obviously still the town's biggest building (**5**).

5 Buck's view of Settle, *c.* 1720, redrawn by Peter Brears. The open frontage of the Folly appears directly below the limestone crag of Castleberg at the centre of this, the earliest depiction of the town.

The West Prospect of Settle in Craven

The Shepherds
Sun Dyal

Scool

P. Brears Sculp.

As was usual, an inventory was made of Preston's goods and a copy lodged with the probate court at York. Whilst inventories do not usually include real estate, a quirk of the land law means that Preston's inventory includes some (but perhaps not all) of his property in Settle including The Folly itself, named as the 'Newhouse' and valued at £200. (The total inventory came to a little under £1500.) More conventionally the inventory gives us a room-by-room account of the house, listing the contents of each room: from the room's name and its contents, we can see how they were used by Preston's household. It is then possible to connect the rooms in the inventory with the rooms of the building as it exists today. All in all we can provide a detailed description of Richard Preston's house at the time of his death, showing how the building was designed to meet the needs of a wealthy household even if the veneer of prosperity sometimes seems to be thin or even lacking. More speculatively, we can show how they may have looked at the time the inventory was made.

Here we discuss every room in turn. Instead of proceeding along the sequence of rooms set out in the inventory, the following description commences at the north door (now the entrance to The Folly's café) and describes that end of the building, before re-entering the central door into the more formal rooms etc. currently open to the public. Finally it will move away from The Folly to explore the contents of Preston's barns. Readers can follow our course round the house through the numbers on (**6**).

1 Kitchen
2 North Parlour
3 Cellar
4 Milk House
5 Back Stairs
6 Maids' Chamber
7 Passage
8 Little Chamber
9 Kitchen Chamber
10 Closet
11 Hall Door
12 Hall
13 Staircase
14 South Parlour
15 Hall Chamber
16 Parlour Chamber

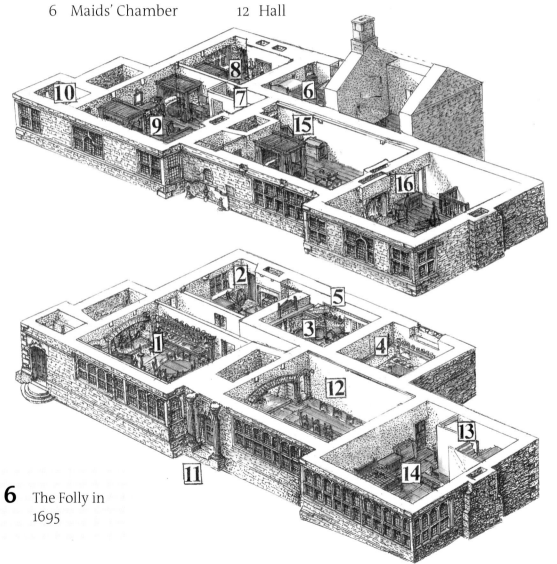

6 The Folly in 1695

7 The Folly in the early eighteenth century, as seen by Peter Brears.

A TOUR OF RICHARD PRESTON'S HOUSE

1 *The Kitchen*

We enter the house through the family's door at the north end of the building and find ourselves in the room – now The Folly café – which the inventory called 'ye Kitching' (**8**). This large room was essentially the family's kitchen/living/dining room, where Lettice, her daughters and maids would have spent much of their time. It was extremely well-lit, with curtained windows along the entire front wall and also partly along the south wall to let the mid-day sun shine into this west-facing room.

Food would have been prepared on one of the tables, probably set beneath three shelves of utensils including skewers, ladles, shears, smoothing irons, a chopping knife, and 'other Iron things [&] Pewther'.

Here large 'havercakes' would have been made by sieving oatmeal through a 'tems' onto a flat wooden bakeboard, ladling on a yeasted oatmeal batter, and swirling it around to form a large, thin cake. In the meantime a smooth slab of stone called a baking stone, probably quarried near Bakestone Beck on the slopes of Fountains Fell, had been heating over the fire on an iron frame called a brig. Once it was hot, the semi-liquid oatcake would have been slid onto its surface to cook through, ready for being eaten fresh and soft, or after it had dried out to perfect crispness.

All the havercakes and other foods prepared on this table were cooked over a fire burning inside the great arched fireplace. The usual local fuel was peat cut from the nearby fells, Richard Preston having a turf cart to bring it down to

8 The kitchen, *c.* 1695. The room also served as the Preston family's dining room.

In her kitchen, Lettice Preston cooked the family's meals using:

1 brass pots
2 brass candlesticks
3 brass mortars
4 brass ladles
5 a clockwork jack
6 iron roasting spits
7 dripping pans
8 fire shovel
9 tongs
10 warming pan
11 flesh forks
12 skewers
13 an axe
14 a chopping knife
15 brigs over the fire
16 shears
17 tossing pan
18 cockle pan
19 chafing dishes
20 bakeboard
21 smoothing iron
22 steel fire-iron
23 reckon crook
24 salt pies
25 sieve
26 silver spoons
27 silver tumbler cups
28 baking stone
29 Three wooden ladles

The bolts used to support the jack (5) used to turn the roasting spits (6) are still to be seen on the arch of the fireplace.

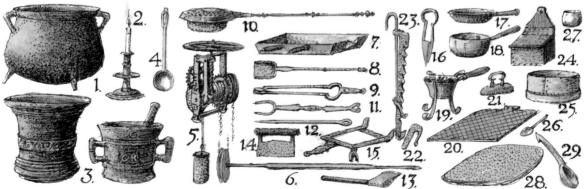

Tanner barn in the early autumn, after it had dried out. He also burned coal (itself a sign of status), probably brought to Settle from the coal pits at Ingleton or Garsdale Head using the two coal sacks noted in the inventory. The peats would burn efficiently either on a hearthstone or in a small portable grate called a chafing dish to give a gentle, almost flameless heat. This was ideal for simmering porridge, joints and stews, frying eggs, bacon, ham and meats, or boiling cockles, in various brass pots and pans, but the radiant heat of coal was essential for roasting. Coal had to be burned in a raised iron grate which, being part of the fixtures of the house, was omitted from the inventory.

Both peat and coal fires were started by striking a steel 'fire-iron' held across the knuckles of one hand against a piece of

flint held in the other to direct sparks onto pieces of scorched linen called tinder. When placed within a handful of dry plant stalks or wood shavings and gently blown, flames appeared, ready to kindle small dried heather stalks or twigs in the fireplace. These in turn set fire to chips of wood neatly chopped with an axe, and finally the peat or coal as it was arranged on top. Once the fire had been built up, adding fuel with tongs and removing ash with a shovel, cooking could begin. Cooking pots were hung over the fire from an adjustable iron device called a reckon hook, frying pans and saucepans were stood over it on the iron brigs, and joints were roasted in front of it on iron spits mounted on spit-racks. In smaller houses the spits were turned by hand until the meat was 'cooked to a turn', but here a clockwork mechanism called a jack was used. Its gears, weight and flywheel were mounted at the right end of the fireplace arch, whilst its drive-shaft passed back through the arch to terminate in a grooved wooden pulley-wheel carrying a loop of iron chain. A similar pulley mounted on the end of a spit hung within the bottom end of the loop, so that the meat constantly rotated before the fire to ensure that it cooked evenly. The fats and juices dropping from the joints fell into dripping pans set beneath, from where they could be ladled up to baste the meat, keeping it succulent and moist. The remaining artefacts found around the fireplace included a hanging wooden box with sloping lid called a 'saltpy' to keep the salt dry and ready for use, a warming pan to be filled with embers to air the beds, and all manner of pots and small utensils too cheap to be individually priced and listed together as 'All other Hustlements of Household stuffe'. The range of household goods in the kitchen is shown in (**8**).

The remainder of the kitchen was furnished as a living-room with a settle in its traditional place between the external door and the fireplace and a small round table called a stand set by its side to hold a brass candlestick and drinks. Other furniture included a chest, three stools, a long-case clock and six chairs set around a dining table. With their table covered with a pristine white linen tablecloth and set with their silver tableware, spoons and tumbler cups, along with their pewter dishes and brass candlesticks, the Prestons would have been able to dine here in great comfort.

9 The North Parlour, *c.* 1695. The staircase to the right of the fireplace led up to the Maids' Chamber, but this was later replaced by the 'beehive' oven, still to be seen here.

2 *The North Parlour*

The room directly behind the kitchen, now the rear room of The Folly's café, was called 'the Parlor' in the inventory (**9**). In the late seventeenth century many large houses had two parlours, one called a 'winter parlour' that functioned almost as a servants' hall, and another furnished in the most opulent manner as a 'state' dining room-cum-bedroom. This parlour in the sunless north-east corner of The Folly was clearly of the 'winter parlour' variety, being used to store food and accommodate servants' beds. Ground oatmeal and dried broad beans were kept in a massive chest called an ark, its lid usually being removable so that when inverted and mounted on a couple of poles it might serve as a hand-barrow for carrying its contents. As the oatmeal was tipped in it was packed down beneath the stockinged feet of a servant, thus ensuring that it did not decay before use. Sometimes hams and flitches of salt-beef and bacon were embedded in the meal, ready for use over the long months of winter, but they were also hung up from hooks in the ceiling, wrapped in linen cloths to keep off the flies. The long wooden salting tub used for curing the beef and bacon was stored in this room, ready for use each autumn.

Despite its fashionable appearance, the fireplace in this room was intended for practical use. Its masonry shows that it had an iron firegrate set in the middle, with a separate grate built into its right-hand side with a flue leading off through the side wall. This was the base or 'furnace' for a still. At this period many fashionable ladies were skilled in the arts of distillation, making their own medicines, liqueurs and scented toilet waters. Lettice's still would probably have been of the 'common' or 'cold' variety. This had a lower section in which the basic ingredients were boiled and a conical pewter upper section in which, when wrapped in cold wet cloths, the steam condensed and the product was collected and run off along a projecting tubular spout. The fireplace here was also provided with a firepan, an iron vessel rather like a saucepan in which the burning coals and peats could be carried off to hearths in other parts of the house whenever additional fires were to be lit.

The 'Two spinning wheels & a sackwebb' stored here show that Lettice, her daughters and maids spun their own flax into yarn, ready for being sent out to a local weaver to make into cloth. The finer fibres produced linen yarn for high quality white tablecloths, sheets and underclothes, while the coarser fibres produced 'harden' yarn for a kind of soft, light-brown sacking used by servants for the same purposes, as well as for hard-wearing aprons and kitchen cloths. The 'sackwebb' would have been a length of this 'harden' material.

With the exception of a table and a chair, the remaining furniture here was designed for servants, most probably Richard's clerks. They would have provided useful overnight security for the household when sleeping here, one in an ordinary bed, and the other in a low 'Trunckle [sic] bedd stead' – a truckle bed on wheels or castors which could be pushed under the higher bed when out of use during the day. Each clerk was probably provided with his own 'little Oake chest' in which to store his personal clothing and effects.

The door in the south side of the parlour led into a pair of low, dark and cold rooms running along the back of The Folly and facing into a narrow passage cut into the face of the native rock. This position made them ideal for storing both artefacts and food.

3 *The Cellar*

The first of these rooms was the cellar (**10**). Cellars were used for storing drinks and could be either above or below ground level, so long as they were cool and dark. This cellar is at ground level, in the coldest part of the house, and has only a tiny window/vent in its back wall. Its floor was paved with neat square flagstones on which stood frames and shelves to hold seven 36-gallon barrels of beer, and bottles probably containing beer and home-made and imported wines. There were also a couple of stools here and two 'Gimlins', shallow tubs in which bacon was salted for preservation. The cellar door would be locked and bolted to keep its contents safe from unauthorised pilfering. When the door was open, the cellar would have served as a buttery for serving drinks to the family in their kitchen, or to visitors and clients in the hall.

10 The Cellar. The door led into the Milk House and the short passage between the Kitchen and Hall.

4 *The Milk House*

The Prestons kept three 'branded', meaning red and brown brindled cows, probably of the Longhorn breed, sufficient to serve their own needs and produce a little surplus for sale. Managing the milk-house (**11**) would have been one of Lettice's responsibilities. Unlike a complete dairy, in which butter and cheese was made, the milkhouse had neither wooden churns nor cheese presses, but only two side frames, whatever they were, two tables, two dishboards (dish-racks), two shelves and a number of earthenware vessels. These vessels would have comprised large, shallow lead-glazed milkpans into which the fresh milk was

11 The Milk House

strained and left overnight for the cream to rise, so that it could be skimmed off into cream pots. Some of it may have been worked in a small earthen churn to make butter for the household, while the remaining skimmed milk was drunk either on its own, or with porridge. Lettice may also have made curds, cream cheeses, syllabubs, and possets for her family and friends. High quality dairy skills were admired at all levels of society at this time.

5 Back Stairs

Returning to the parlour, a staircase by the side of the fireplace – later replaced by an oven – led up into the maids' chamber in a mezzanine over the cellar.

6 The Maids' Chamber

This was where the maids slept, its two oak chests and two boxes along with a trunk, suggesting that two maids shared its single bed, an accepted practice in most households. At the head of the stair from the parlour a few steps rose up through the adjacent wall into a passage that ran alongside the little chamber to provide backstairs access to all the first-floor chambers. Such backstairs were intended solely for the use of the servants, and were of very recent introduction. As the architectural historian Marc Girouard commented, one of their main benefits was that 'the gentry walking up the [main] stairs no longer met their last night's faeces coming down them'.

7 The Passage

The location of the passage is uncertain. It was furnished with a desk, a little table, two oak clothes-presses (wardrobes), and a great oak chest, another chest and a trunk for the storage of the household linens. Some were for use on the dining table; 'five fine, nine coarser and two diaper tablecloths' and '72 fine, 72 huckaback and 18 plain canvas napkins' whilst others were for the beds; '18 pair linen, 31 pair canvas (servants') and one large Holland (fine Dutch-woven linen) sheets'; '16 pair pillowbears (pillowcases)' and for washing; 'three towels'

This large stock of linen, valued at £21 12*s*., may appear excessive for a household of around ten adults and three children, but is not unusual at this period. Representing an enormous investment in time and money, it was valuable in its own right, often representing a major part of a young woman's dowry. It should also be remembered that wash-days tended to be undertaken relatively infrequently during the course of a year, so that used sheets etc. accumulated over a number of weeks before being laundered and returned to their chest ready for use.

8 *The Little Chamber*

Located directly over the north parlour, the little chamber was furnished as a comfortable bedroom, kept warm by a fire with a fire shovel and fender, and curtains at the window. It housed only one bed, the presence of 'A Lookeing glasse' suggesting that it was occupied by one (or possibly two) of the Preston daughters.

9 *The Kitchen Chamber*

Receiving its name from its position over the kitchen, this chamber was The Folly's best bedroom where Richard and Lettice Preston would have slept. It appears to have been furnished in a fashionable manner, with a pair of good quality beds flanked by two little tables and two tall, narrow candle-sticks. Six upholstered chairs would

have lined the walls, with a comfortable 'wanded' or wicker chair probably set by the fire shovel and tongs at the fireside. A close-stool or commode was provided for overnight use, with another looking glass with which Lettice would have made herself presentable each morning.

10 *The Closet*

In seventeenth-century parlance, a 'closet' was a small, private inner room, sometimes used as a study or for keeping accounts and personal papers. Leading off the north-west corner of the kitchen chamber, Richard's closet was ideal for this purpose, being securely separated from the bustle of the household and illuminated by two walls of windows that overlooked the surrounding streets. A broad shelved recess provided storage for boxes of papers etc. The inventory shows that the room contained a desk and boxes: more oddly it also contained £1 6*s*. 8*d*. of wheat.

This completes the sequence of rooms used by the family. Our tour now returns into the road to re-enter The Folly by its main door into the hall, and continues through the remaining ground- and first-floor rooms.

11 *The Main Door*

The masonry of the main doorcase is of exceptional quality, featuring rare tapered and fluted columns and an elaborate door-head dated 1679 (**12**). Its most unusual feature, however, is an easily-missed shallow round boss carved at the centre of its underside. This bears a complex design of interlaced circles cut in low relief, and was probably intended to serve as a safeguard against witchcraft. Similarly tangled motifs were often chalked on hearthstones to protect the inhabitants from evil influences descending from the chimneys (**23**).

The door itself, like the external kitchen door, appears to be original, with a framed and panelled construction and strong internal iron hinges. Instead of opening onto a wide cross-passage as found in most large houses up to the middle of the seventeenth century, it enters a small porch further protected by an internal door. This fashionable 'baffle entry' at the side of the main fireplace was extremely convenient, giving direct access to clients entering the hall while maintaining the privacy of the family's north wing.

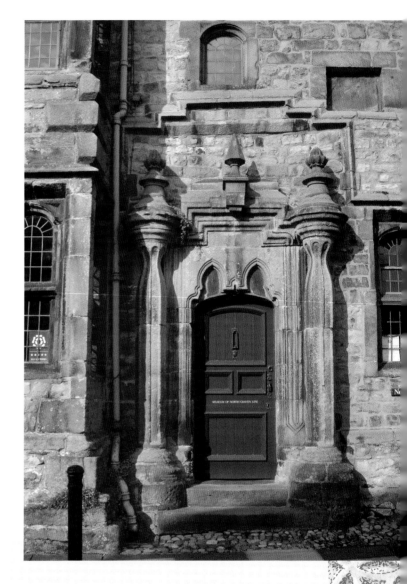

12 The Main Door. As the 'public' entrance to the house, this led directly into the Hall from the main road.

12 *The Hall*

In houses of this date halls were losing their traditional role as the main living/dining area for servants, but still continued to serve as the principal rooms in which visitors were received. Only the most important would be invited into the higher-status rooms beyond. In order to create an initial impression of substantial prosperity, the hall (**13**) displayed The Folly's finest architectural features. A huge nine-light mullioned window (the southern-most light of which is blocked), with carved corbels, ran along its western wall facing the road, while to the north one of the grandest fireplaces in the Dales was flanked by symmetrical arched doorways, one from the porch and the other into the kitchen. The fireplace itself has its jambs carved with elaborate mouldings that match those of the oak ceiling beams above, while its arch is made up of joggle-jointed voussoirs, the back of each one being identified (on the reverse) by its own Arabic numeral (**14**). In 1695 it housed only a 'fire Iron' to strike sparks from a flint for firelighting and an iron girdle. This suggests that it usually had a peat fire burning on its hearth to warm the hall, with oatcakes sometimes being baked over its gentle heat. The central section of the eastern wall opened up over the cellar to provide a broad, deep and impressive stairwell illuminated by its own six-light mullioned window. The broad treads, shallow pitch, massive newel-posts and finely-turned spiral banisters of the staircase itself all combine to provide a sense of stately elegance, immediately suggesting that it gave access to far finer rooms above.

Since the hall was essentially Richard's business room where he and his two clerks would meet clients, it was simply but comfortably furnished with two long tables, a form, six joined chairs provided with cushions and a stool covered in green upholstery.

13 The Hall *c.*1695

14 The Hall Fireplace. This is surely one of the region's finest vernacular fireplaces. Each stone of its joggled arch is individually numbered on the back to ensure that the masons erected them in the correct order. To the right, a passageway with its own door leads through to the family's quarters.

As we have already mentioned, the question about the hall is whether it always had the staircase (**15**) rising from its back which is now such a prominent feature of the room or whether the wall was breached at a later date, the staircase tower added and the staircase inserted. In (**6**) the rear walls of the hall and the hall chamber over it are shown in what may have been their original form without the stairs, but to help understand this part of the building the base of the hall tower is shown in what may have been its original form in the first phase of the house.

Above the ceiling over the staircase is a prospect room giving extensive views overlooking the Ribble Valley, which was added either in the second phase of building or even later, but by about 1720. This is a small tower, best seen

15 The Staircase

16 The Folly's tower, seen from behind the building.

from behind and above The Folly (**16**). It is unlikely that there was ever an internal staircase to it, and it may be that access was always by a wall-mounted ladder and through a trap door.

13 *South Staircase*

The pattern of ceiling joists in the South Parlour shows that there was a staircase in the corner of the room giving access to the South Parlour Chamber over it.

The question is whether this was an original feature of the building to mirror the private staircase rising out of the rear parlour. The staircase may be seen in the photograph of the room taken in 1971 (**21**). It was a wooden staircase whose plain and unadorned construction suggest that it was inserted when the house was divided into tenements in the nineteenth century.

14 *The South Parlour*

Entered from the hall, the south parlour was intended to be the most opulent room in the house. At this date parlours were usually a combination of principal bedroom and dining room, where the finest fixtures and fittings were displayed. Unfortunately its original fireplace has been removed, but its thirty-two light mullioned window extending from the north wall, along the entire west wall and one-third of the south wall still impresses today. Some of the windows in the south-western corner are 1970s work, made to replace windows destroyed when a door was made into the room, as may be seen in (**21**), doubtless at the same time as the staircase was inserted.

In a house of this size and quality we would expect a richly moulded plaster ceiling and finely panelled walls, but there is no evidence that these were ever installed.

The logic of the building is that this, the single most impressive room, was Preston's private room, but by the time the inventory was taken the south parlour was little more than a junk room housing two cheap beds, three old chests, a side table, a form, two sides of a dismantled ark '& other old things in ye same room', all valued at a mere £2.

15 *The Hall Chamber*

Located directly over the hall, the hall chamber should have been a well-appointed bedroom. It housed the best bed in the house, one that was three times the value of most of the others, along with an ark, two oak chests, a square table, a screen, a green-upholstered stool and four little boxes. The small window in the west wall was to light a closet placed between it and the chimney stack rising from the hall fireplace, but if this was ever constructed, it has been removed.

16 *The South Parlour Chamber*

Again, given its prestigious position, its size, the light coming from mullioned windows in three walls and a fireplace, this fine bedchamber served only as a junk-room when the inventory was made.

Its contents comprised two cupboards, a long chest, a chair, two scuttles, a portable winch called a crab, a middleboard for the bottom of a cart and a cart axle. This all adds to the impression that the house was in some disarray at the time of Preston's death.

This ends the tour of Richard Preston's house as described in his inventory of 1696. As we noted before, there is no mention of the rooms on the second floor. Instead the inventory continues with the Brewhouse. We should not be surprised that The Folly had its own brewhouse: it is a further reflection of the house's status as a gentleman's residence. It is now recognised that poorer people bought their beer where richer ones brewed for their household. The brewhouse appears to have occupied the outbuilding adjoining the north end of The Folly. Now converted into a garage, early photographs show a chimney on its end wall that probably carried off the smoke from the brewing coppers below. Its contents are described as 'Brewing vessels and other wood vessel' along with a 52½ -gallon hogshead and nine 36-gallon

barrels temporarily stored in the north parlour, while seven more barrels were kept in the cellar. The total capacity of 576 gallons may seem excessive for a household of some six adults and their visitors, but since beer was their everyday drink, and at least four pints a day of varying strengths was quite normal, it represents about six months' consumption.

Richard Preston grew his own barley, storing it in arks in his barns, converting it into malt and drying it on a 'Hare' (i.e. horse-hair) cloth in his own kiln. From here it was kept in the north parlour ready for use. The hops would have been bought in, while there was a plentiful supply of fresh hard water from the town's well, a series of troughs immediately outside the back gate. Home-brewing was usually undertaken by a skilled maid, but Preston may have called on the services of an experienced male or female brewer to undertake the periodic brewing process.

The inventory says little about the lands of the deceased, but it does list the contents of Preston's two barns and this allows us some insight into Preston's farming activities. Of the two, we can guess that Tanner Barn was nearer to The Folly. Here Richard Preston kept a heifer and two milch-cows, all of a brindled or mixed red-brown colour. Their milk would have been carried to The Folly's milkhouse.

The stable section housed a sorrel mare, an old horse and an old pacing horse, for which there were three hackney (riding) saddles and bridles, and a couple of colts. Three load- or pack-saddles, with four sacks, two coal sacks, an overlay and a wantey (a girth to tie the pack-saddle in place) enabled the horses to carry relatively small loads. For larger loads they were harnessed with padded collars called 'Barkehams', having stiff hames from which traces passed back to a cart, and a cart harness called 'trappings' including a cart-saddle to protect the horse's back from the backband that supported the cartshafts.

A single hog lived in the swinecote, for, being January, its companions were now bacon in the north parlour. In the chamber above were planks, joists, miscellaneous wood, a garden spade, a sickle, and an ox-hide whip called a 'lain'. Elsewhere at the barn sheaves of oats and barley still to be threshed probably stood in stacks, the

grain that had already been threshed and winnowed being stored in an ark, ready to be taken to the mill and ground into meal. About seventy yards of hay remained in the lofts to feed the cows and horses, along with dried peat ('turf') for heating The Folly.

We can deduce that Yeoman barn was further away. Of his two barns, this one was more convenient for his pastures, meadows and cultivated lands. Here Preston kept his herd of seven heifers before they calved and a single cow, along with four little steers (bullocks) and six oxen. The oxen usually served as draught animals for at least four or five years before being slaughtered as beef. Working in pairs linked by strong wooden yokes over their shoulders and U-shaped bows around their necks, they were linked to a plough or harrow by a chain called a team that had a ring at one end and a hook at the other. The plough itself was made of wood, only the sharp vertical coulter and the pointed horizontal share being of iron, along with the top of the ploughstaff with which the ploughman cleared away any turf, roots or stones that got caught between the coulter and share. A mare and a horse kept here were also used to pull a plough and 'other Implements of Husbandry' by means of rope traces hooked from their collars back to horizontal bars called swingle trees, and on to the front of the implement with an iron 'team'.

A small flock of thirteen ewes and a lamb grazed around this barn, probably receiving a little hay over the winter months. Most of the 'forty yards of hay' stored here would have been used to feed the cattle as they remained in their stalls over the coldest months of winter. A 'coupe' or muck-cart was used to carry their manure into the fields, where it would be spread, while a turf-cart brought in dried peats from the moors.

Sadly there are things that the inventory fails to tell us. It does not, for instance, include any list of Preston's books although one assumes him to be an educated man, and, as a lawyer, frequently in York and London, he had the opportunity to keep abreast of the latest printed works.

17 The Folly in our own times:
a view by Richard Carman.

THE LATER HISTORY

One would guess that Dawson's reason for buying The Folly was that he wanted to continue – or revive – Preston's legal practice. But once he inherited Langcliffe Hall and moved there, he had no need for the house. It is possible that it was settled on the son of his second marriage because he expected him to use the house, but there is no sign that the junior line of the Dawsons ever saw The Folly (or Settle Hall as they called it) as other than an encumbrance. The problem it posed can be seen in an advertisement that appeared in the Leeds paper late in 1780 (**18**): the house would be suitable for two families or might be converted into a manufactory (making textiles). Around a decade later the decision was taken to turn The Folly into a farm and land was bought to be tenanted with the house. Thereafter it is possible to trace a succession of farming tenants. In 1818 the

the fame.

SETTLE-HALL.

To be LETT, and enter'd upon immediately,

Situate in SETTLE,

A Large DWELLING-HOUSE, known by the Name of SETTLE-HALL, containing three Stories in Height, and from six to more spacious Rooms on each Floor, of various Dimensions, from twelve Feet by twelve Feet, to nineteen Feet by twenty-seven Feet, comprizing every Convenience for one or two separate Families, would be very suitable for a Manufactory, and may be had on very moderate Terms.

Enquire of Messrs. Birkbeck, in Settle; or of Mr Cookson, in Leeds.

To be LETT,

TAYLOR'S REFRESHMENT ROOMS,
The Folly, SETTLE.

Tea, Coffee,
AND
Refreshments
SUPPLIED AT SHORT NOTICE ON
REASONABLE TERMS.

GOOD ACCOMMODATION
FOR TOURISTS.

WELL-AIRED BEDS. HOT & COLD BATHS.
ÆRATED WATERS.
Pork & Veal Pies in season.

18 This advertisement for The Folly, here called 'Settle Hall' appeared in the *Leeds Intelligencer* in December 1780.

19 Taylor's Refreshment Rooms: an advertisement of *c.*1895.

tenancy of Settle Hall Farm was advertised with 449 acres of land. The farmer though was not promised the use of the whole house. The 1841 census shows that the tenant was William Hardacre: in 1851 he was still tenant and was said to be farming 124 acres.

The census also shows that parts of the house were let to other families throughout the century. There were always three or more families in the building in the censuses between 1861 and 1901, and a variety of transient boarders and lodgers. This long period when The Folly was little more than a tenement has left its mark in the plain fireplaces in some of its rooms, and instances of graffiti made by residents or employees who were bored. At some time an additional entrance into the building was made by inserting a doorway through the windows at the south end of the house and a staircase made to rise out of the south parlour to give access to the rooms above. (**21**)

The last of the Settle Hall farmers was William Bowskill, farming there in 1891, but by 1901 he had given up the farm and was working as a cab proprietor in Morecambe. Thereafter The Folly was

invented again. From around 1894 the north part of the building was used as refreshment rooms, first Taylor's Refreshment Rooms (**19**) and then, when Robert Taylor moved on, he was succeeded by Thomas Marsden. In fact the refreshment rooms also offered beds and accommodation, in Taylor's case 'well aired beds' as well as hot and cold baths. (Whether there was any demand for cold baths is unrecorded, alas.) After Marsden, the north end of the building was used as a fish and chip shop. The conversion of the north wing in modern times into first a holiday let and more recently a café merely proves that there is nothing new!

Fish and chips proved not to be the future. From around 1909 the northern and central part of the house was used by the Grisedales, over several generations joiners and cabinet makers. In the 1911 census, James Grisedale and his wife had three children, but their household also contained a nephew, a niece and a middle-aged boarder. They also sold a range of furnishings including beds and carpets, and there are photographs in which their stock is shown piled outside and hanging from windows, doubtless to illustrate the range of their wares. (**20**).

20 The Folly, *c.* 1925, with Grisedale's stock being displayed.

As for the remainder of the house, we have reports that it was being used in the 1890s by the Settle Young Mens' Friendly Society and for classes held by Settle church. This may simply be the hall being rented by the hour. The 1901 census suggests that the south end of The Folly was still in multiple occupancy. This changed from about 1906 when the tenants became the Ecclestons, originally called 'marine store dealers', but best thought of as second-hand dealers. Their shop seems to have been the old brewhouse at the north end of The Folly. In 1911 three generations of Ecclestons were living in the south end of the house: William sen. aged 60 and his son William jun. aged 30, their wives and William junior's two children.

We gain particular insights into The Folly at this period of its history from the survey made of it for taxation purposes immediately before the First World War. The Valuation Officer commented on the poor state of repair of the roof. The Ecclestons had a living room, sitting room, kitchen and scullery on the ground floor, three bedrooms on the first floor and two bedrooms and a lumber room on the top floor. They also had a storeroom with loft over and a lean-to store room, 'in very bad condition' and used as a marine stores adjoining The Folly at the north end. The Grisedale share of the house had a living room and sitting room (the latter with a large arched fireplace) and a kitchen and scullery on the ground floor, Above there were four bedrooms and a bathroom and on the second floor three bedrooms. They used the hall as a shop and showroom and had a storeroom and a joiner's workshop on the top floor.

The Ecclestons remained at The Folly until 1956 and then the south end of the house stood empty for a number of years. (For its state in 1971 see (**21**)). The Grisedales remained in business until about 1966. The problem of how to use The Folly was resolved for a time by the decision of the late Philip Dawson to move to Settle and live in The Folly. Dawson also had aspirations that part of the house should be used as Settle library or developed as a museum. A report of January 1964 says that the south end remained unoccupied and was dilapidated: Dawson complained that its windows were repeatedly broken.

21 The South Parlour, 1971, showing the door into
The Folly from the road and the now removed
staircase. Image from the photographic survey by
the Royal Commission on Historical Monuments.

None of Dawson's aspirations came to pass in his lifetime. In the early 1970s part of the ground floor was used for a time as a doctors' surgery and consulting rooms before the opening of the Town Head surgery. In 1971 a photographic survey was made of the house: the interior pictures showing just how shabby it then was, and revealing features which have since been removed, such as the wall and door at the top of the stairs. As a bachelor, Dawson far from filled it and in 1983 he sold The Folly to an antiques dealer. In 1990 the house was sold again as two dwellings. The central part and southern part of the building was acquired by the North Craven Building Preservation Trust in 1996 and opened after repair and refurbishment in 2001 (**22**). In 2010 the north end was also acquired by the Trust, bringing the two parts of the building again into single ownership but now with a public purpose, to preserve and protect The Folly for the future.

22 HRH the Prince of Wales with Alan Bennett at the opening of the Museum of North Craven Life in The Folly, 2001 seen with Patricia Simpson, Anne Read and Cllr Beth Graham.

FURTHER READING

The Folly awaits a definitive guide to its history and building (should such a thing ever be possible). Professor Richard Hoyle is preparing a full account of Richard Preston and his house: it is envisaged that this will appear in the *Yorkshire Archaeological Journal*. This will include a full account of Preston's legal difficulties: it will also print his inventory. This guide has also drawn on the materials on the later history of the house gathered by Sarah Lister with contributions from Pamela Jordan. The house has previously been described in architectural terms in reports by Kirsty Rodwell (1995) and Alison Armstrong and Arnold Pacey (2003). Copies of both reports can be consulted at The Folly by arrangement. The full range of photographs of The Folly taken by the Royal Commission on Historical Monuments in 1971 can be seen through the Historic England website.

A NOTE TO OUR READERS

The North Craven Building Preservation Trust (Charity no. 505438) was founded in 1976 to preserve and promote the built heritage of North Craven and to acquire local collections, providing public access to them through its ownership and management of the Museum of North Craven Life.

The Grade One-listed Folly is the Trust's flagship project, but its rescue, restoration and day-to-day running is a huge and ongoing undertaking. Two thirds of the building was purchased in 1996 with support from the Heritage Lottery Fund, but it was not until 2010 that the acquisition of the north range enabled the two parts of the house to be reunited. Much still remains to be done before the Trust's ambition of opening the whole of this exciting and mysterious building for everyone to visit and enjoy can be fully realised.

As the Trust receives no income from either local or national government, it is reliant on generating its own income. It exists only because of the energy, commitment and determination of its volunteers and supporters. We can offer many openings for those who wish to join us, and we welcome donations and bequests from those who cherish this house as much as we do and share our aims of preserving it for the future whilst making it accessible to the people of north Craven and beyond.

For further information visit www.thefolly.org.uk.

23 Until the nineteenth century there was a belief that entwined motifs prevented evil entering a house. The Folly contains three such devices showing that even high status individuals were not immune from what we would regard as superstition. The middle design above is carved just above the door into the hall, while those to the left and right are carved over the kitchen and south parlour windows.